I0793954

NATIVE AMERICAN NATIONS

Hopi

F.A. BIRD

Checkerboard Library

An Imprint of Abdo Publishing
abdobooks.com

ABDOBOOKS.COM

Published by Abdo Publishing, a division of ABDO, PO Box 398166, Minneapolis, Minnesota 55439.
Copyright © 2025 by Abdo Consulting Group, Inc. International copyrights reserved in all countries. No part of this book may be reproduced in any form without written permission from the publisher. Checkerboard Library™ is a trademark and logo of Abdo Publishing.

Printed in the United States of America, North Mankato, Minnesota
102024
012025

THIS BOOK CONTAINS RECYCLED MATERIALS

Editor: Lauri Nelson
Design: Mighty Media, Inc.

Cover Photograph: Albuquerque Journal/AP Photo
Interior Photographs: Ad_hominem/Shutterstock Images, p. 7; Angel Wynn/DanitaDelimont.com/ "Danita Delimont Photography"/Newscom, p. 11; Angel Wynn/NativeStock, pp. 21, 23; CORBIS/Corbis via Getty Images, p. 15; Evans/Three Lions/Getty Images, p. 25; John Cancalosi/Minden Pictures, p. 29; Keystone View Company/FPG/Archive Photos/Hulton Archive/Getty Images, p. 9; National Museum of the American Indian, Smithsonian Institution (24/2372 and 23/2467). Photos by NMAI Photo Services, p. 13; National Museum of the American Indian, Smithsonian Institution (24/3125). Photo by NMAI Photo Services, p. 19; Ross D. Franklin/AP Photo, p. 27; The Protected Art Archive/ Alamy Stock Photo, p. 17; ventdusud/Shutterstock Images, p. 5

Library of Congress Control Number: 2024938811

Publisher's Cataloging-in-Publication Data
Names: Bird, F.A., author.
Title: Hopi / by F.A. Bird
Description: Minneapolis, Minnesota : ABDO Publishing, 2025 | Series: Native American nations | Includes online resources and index.
Identifiers: ISBN 9781098296223 (lib. bdg.) | ISBN 9798384917335 (ebook)
Subjects: LCSH: Hopi Indians--Juvenile literature. | Moki Indians--Juvenile literature. | Native Americans--Juvenile literature. | Indians of North America--Juvenile literature. | Indigenous peoples--Social life and customs--Juvenile literature. | Cultural anthropology--Juvenile literature.
Classification: DDC 973.0497--dc23

Contents

CHAPTER 1

Homelands

The name Hopi comes from the word *Hopituh* or *Hopiikwa*, which means "Peaceful People" in the Hopi language. The Hopi spoke a language in the Shoshonean branch of the Uto-Aztecan language family.

The Hopi lived on the Colorado **Plateau** in northern Arizona. The Colorado Plateau is centered on the Four Corners region of the southwestern United States. This land had canyons, deserts, mountain ranges, high mountain peaks, and **mesas**. Water was scarce. It came from melted snow, summer rains, and underground springs.

Today, the Hopi live on three sandstone mesas on the Colorado Plateau. The mesas rise above the desert floor. The Hopi build their homes on the mesas' flat tops. They farm on the desert floor and on terraces below the mesas.

Hopi Point in the Grand Canyon is named after the Hopi Tribe who have lived in the area for thousands of years.

CHAPTER 2

Society

The Hopi villages were called First, Second, and Third Mesa. First Mesa was home to the Walpi, Tewa, and Sichomovi villages. Second Mesa consisted of the Shongopavi, Mishongnovi, and Shipaulovi villages. Third Mesa included the Hotevilla, Bacavi, Moencopi, Kykotsmovi, and Oraibi villages.

In the villages, Hopi society was bound by **clans**. There were many Hopi clans. Each clan had special duties. They performed ceremonies to give thanks. The ceremonies kept harmony between the Hopi and the natural world.

The Hopi held some ceremonies in public **plazas**. Criers told other villages when ceremonies would take place. Other Hopi ceremonies were held privately in underground chambers called **kivas**.

Each Hopi village had a high priest, a priest, clan chiefs, and war chiefs. Women were spiritual leaders, too. Their duties were to keep the peace, protect the people, and continue the traditional teachings.

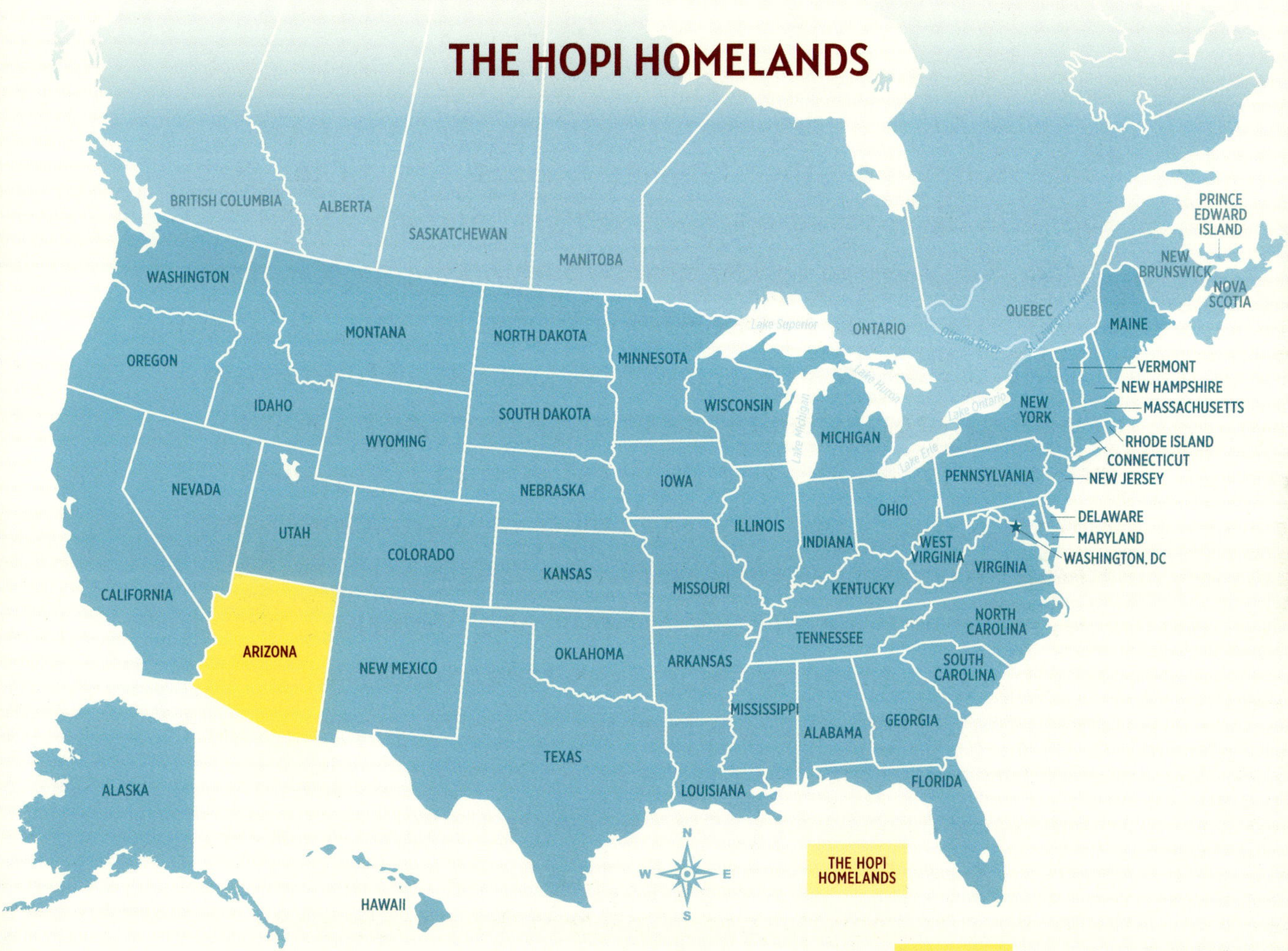
THE HOPI HOMELANDS
BRITISH COLUMBIA
ALBERTA
SASKATCHEWAN
MANITOBA
ONTARIO
QUEBEC
PRINCE EDWARD ISLAND
NEW BRUNSWICK
NOVA SCOTIA
Lake Superior
Lake Michigan
Lake Huron
Lake Ontario
Lake Erie
Ottawa River
St. Lawrence River
WASHINGTON
OREGON
IDAHO
MONTANA
NORTH DAKOTA
SOUTH DAKOTA
MINNESOTA
WISCONSIN
MICHIGAN
NEW YORK
MAINE
VERMONT
NEW HAMPSHIRE
MASSACHUSETTS
RHODE ISLAND
CONNECTICUT
NEW JERSEY
PENNSYLVANIA
DELAWARE
MARYLAND
WASHINGTON, DC
WYOMING
NEVADA
UTAH
COLORADO
NEBRASKA
IOWA
ILLINOIS
INDIANA
OHIO
WEST VIRGINIA
VIRGINIA
KENTUCKY
CALIFORNIA
KANSAS
MISSOURI
ARIZONA
NEW MEXICO
OKLAHOMA
ARKANSAS
TENNESSEE
NORTH CAROLINA
SOUTH CAROLINA
MISSISSIPPI
ALABAMA
GEORGIA
TEXAS
LOUISIANA
FLORIDA
ALASKA
HAWAII
N
S
E
W
THE HOPI HOMELANDS

CHAPTER 3

Homes

Hopi women built their families' houses. They built homes made from stones such as flagstone and sandstone. Women set the stones with adobe mortar, and covered them with a thick layer of mud and clay.

They covered the roofs and floors with tamarack brush and rabbit grass. Then the women covered the roofs with a layer of clay two and a half feet (1 m) thick. They also covered the walls with a thick layer of clay. The clay kept the houses cool in summer and warm in winter.

Hopi families lived in the upper stories of the house. The bottom story was for storage. They hung dried wild teas and tobacco from the roof beams.

Women built the houses close together and on top of each other. The Hopi used ladders to move from story to story in these multilevel homes. They made the ladders from juniper and pine wood. They tied the rungs to the ladder with rope woven from plant fibers.

Hopi people among their adobe home. Adobe is a building material made from sun-dried earth and straw.

CHAPTER 4

Food

Hopi villagers gathered, hunted, and farmed. They gathered wild tea, wild spinach, acorns, and piñon nuts.

Hopi men hunted in the mountains and deserts. They used bows and arrows to hunt deer, bighorn sheep, pronghorn, bear, rabbit, and wild turkey. Hopi men also used hand-woven snares to trap small animals and birds.

The Hopi practiced **dry farming**. The men cleared space for fields at the foot of the **mesas**. They used a planting stick to make holes in the soil. Next, the men placed seeds in each hole. As the corn grew, they weeded the fields with wooden hoes. Early crops were watered with melted snow.

The women planted gardens in terraces that lined the mesas. Until the rains came, they watered these terrace gardens with buckets of water from natural springs.

The Hopi also planted beans, squash, and melons. Later, the Europeans brought peaches, pumpkins, apricots, and grapes. The Hopi also raised sheep and cattle.

Hopi women make Piki bread from finely ground blue corn, water, and ashes from a burned juniper bush.

CHAPTER 5

Clothing

Hopi men made clothing from animal skins and woven cloth. They wove cloth from plant and animal fibers. Later, Spanish explorers brought sheep to the region. The Hopi then wove cloth from sheep's wool.

Women and girls wore a rectangular-shaped dress called a manta. It covered the right shoulder, while the left shoulder was bare. They wore a wide, woven **sash** around their waists. Women wore moccasins with leather wraps. The wraps wound around the ankle up to the mid-calf.

Men and boys traditionally wore woven shirts, leggings, and a **kilt** or **breechcloth**. Men also wrapped sashes around their waists. Sometimes they wore a sash across their chest, too. Men wore ankle-high moccasins with light-colored soles.

The Hopi decorated their clothing with colors and symbols that represented nature and their **culture**. They also wore shell and turquoise jewelry.

Hopi men's embroidered shirts

CHAPTER 6

Crafts

The Hopi created many kinds of arts and crafts. They carved kachina dolls and wove baskets. They also made bows and arrows, **rabbit sticks**, gourd rattles, and jewelry.

The Hopi carved kachina dolls from cottonwood tree roots. Kachina dolls represented the supernatural beings in Hopi **culture**. There were more than a hundred different kachinas. Crow Mother, Longhair, and White Corn Maiden are a few.

The Hopi outfitted each kachina doll with the type of clothing, masks, headdresses, and other items used by the kachina during ceremonial dances. A Hopi carver needed to be very knowledgeable about his culture to create a doll that was true to their traditions.

Hopi women wove beautiful baskets. They used yucca to make sifter and coil baskets. They also used wicker and rabbit brush to make plaques.

Nampeyo was one of the finest Hopi potters. She was born on First Mesa, which is known for its pottery.

CHAPTER 7

Family

A Hopi family includes the people of the entire clan. Hopi clans are matrilineal. This means that children belong to their mother's clan. The women of a clan owned its gardens, homes, and possessions.

Children received their names from their father's clan. This happened during a naming ceremony. This was done so that the children had an extended family to protect and teach them throughout life.

Hopi were not allowed to marry members of their own clan. Once a woman agreed to marry, men from the groom's clan wove her wedding clothes. They made two sets of clothing. They rolled the second set in a reed bundle and gave it to the bride. This was called a wedding suitcase. The woman wore these clothes at her death.

Families had to keep the Hopi traditional teachings alive. They required people to be humble, work in cooperation, and respect and protect Mother Earth.

Three young women grinding corn. Their butterfly-whorl hairstyle shows that they are old enough to be married.

CHAPTER 8

Children

Hopi children learned from their parents, grandparents, aunts and uncles, clan elders, and religious leaders. They learned Hopi dances, songs, and **culture** as a part of their daily lives.

Women taught the girls how to cook, grind corn, and care for babies. The girls played with kachina dolls. The dolls taught the girls about the different kachinas and the Hopi culture.

Men taught the boys traditional Hopi ways. The boys learned how to make and use **rabbit sticks** and bows and arrows. They painted their bows with the traditional white, blue, yellow, and purple stripes.

Boys and girls played games to develop their minds and bodies. One popular game was darts. They made the darts from corn cobs, and tied feathers on the end. The children threw the darts at a target.

Kachina doll with traditional clothing and butterfly-whorl hair decoration

CHAPTER 9

Traditions

The Hopi emergence story tells how the Hopi came to this world. In the First World, Dawa and Spider Woman created human beings. The humans were told to pray to the gods, take care of the land, and use only what they needed. When the humans forgot to follow these instructions, Dawa destroyed the First World.

The Second World was also destroyed because the humans did not pray or care for the land. When they forgot again in the Third World, Dawa told the humans to go down into the **kivas** to find a new place to live.

The men prayed and were visited by different birds and animals that would later become the **clans**. The animals helped the people climb to an opening above them. The Hopi entered the Fourth World.

Today, the Hopi believe they are living in the Fourth World. They are caretakers, and not owners, of the land. They must continue to pray and dance as Dawa instructed.

Rock carving located at the Hopi Cultural Center. The spiral means the center of the universe.

CHAPTER 10

War

The Hopi are a peaceful people. They do not like war. Their spiritual beliefs taught the Hopi to live in harmony with other people and nature.

The Hopi's remote location on the **mesas** helped keep them safe from outsiders. From the top of the mesas, the Hopi could see a long distance. They could easily see approaching enemies.

From time to time, the Hopi had to protect themselves from hostile tribes. Often the Hopi had to defend themselves against Apache and Navajo **raids**. These tribes robbed Hopi villages. They captured women and children, and sold them into slavery.

In 1680, the Hopi joined Pueblo tribes to fight the Spaniards. The Spaniards wanted to control the Hopi and convert them to Christianity. The Hopi fought to protect their land and **culture**. Many people died. This war is known today as the Pueblo Revolt.

Hopi rawhide shield. The painted designs are from an ancient city called Old Oraibi.

CHAPTER II

Contact with Europeans

The Spaniards were the first Europeans to make contact with the Hopi. In the 1540s, Spanish explorer Francisco Vásquez de Coronado came looking for cities that were full of gold. He did not find them on Hopi lands.

The United States acquired Hopi homelands from the Spaniards. **Raids** into their lands by the Navajo continued. Hopi leaders asked the US government for help. In 1851, the US built Fort Defiance. The fort protected white settlers and protected the Hopi from Navajo raids.

During the Civil War, the US abandoned the fort. The Navajo raids began again. The raids threatened the Hopi's survival, so they asked for help again. The US government did not understand what the Hopi wanted. They were treated rudely and imprisoned. Many Hopi died from hunger and diseases the soldiers brought to their land.

Herd of Hopi goats and sheep in Arizona. The Hopi received sheep through their trades with the Spanish.

CHAPTER 12

Yokiuma

Yokiuma was keeper of the sacred stone tablet. His duty was to protect and maintain the sacred teachings of the Hopi people. Yokiuma and his followers fought against American interference in the Hopi **culture**. So, the US government called them Hostiles. Hopi who went along with the government's programs were called Friendlies.

Yokiuma and his followers did not want to send Hopi children away to American boarding schools. Children at the schools were not allowed to visit home. Yokiuma feared the children would forget the Hopi language and culture. This endangered the Hopi way of life.

The Friendlies and the Hostiles argued in the Hopi villages. This tension in the Oraibi village led to the creation of a new village called Hotevilla.

Hopi culture has survived due to leaders like Yokiuma. Although Yokiuma has died, his wish to protect the Hopi way of life continues in Hotevilla.

Heard Museum World Championship Hoop Dance Contest in Phoenix, Arizona. Hopi dancer Moontee Sinquah says he dances most importantly for his ancestors who fought for his people to be here.

CHAPTER 13

The Hopi Today

In 1882, US President Chester A. Arthur created the Hopi Reservation. It covers more than 1.5 million acres of land. Today, over 14,500 members of the Hopi tribe live there.

In 1936, the Hopi Tribal Council was established. This form of government has a **constitution** like the US Constitution, and it is recognized by the US government.

Today, Hopi children attend schools on the **mesas**. They participate in community activities. To preserve their **culture**, the Hopi do not allow photographs to be taken of their villages or ceremonies. To help preserve their language, the Hopi have written a dictionary with over 30,000 words. Children also learn their language in school.

Many Hopi go to **urban** areas to find work. They return to the mesas for ceremonies. Some Hopi parents have created dance groups. They teach the urban Hopi children dances, songs, and other Hopi cultural ways. This way, the modern Hopi people maintain their traditional way of life.

Hopi girl dressed to perform a social dance.

Glossary

breechcloth—a piece of hide or cloth, usually worn by men, that is wrapped between the legs and tied with a belt around the waist.

clan—a group of families in a community that has a common ancestor.

constitution—the laws that govern a country.

culture—the customs, arts, and tools of a nation or people at a certain time.

dry farming—farming on nonirrigated land by planting drought-resistant crops and turning under soil wet with dew or rain.

kilt—a skirt worn by men that reaches to the knees.

kiva—a ceremonial structure that is usually round and partly underground.

mesa—a flat-topped hill or mountain with steep sides.

plateau—a raised area of flat land.

plaza—a public square or open space in a community.

rabbit stick—a weapon thrown at a running rabbit's legs that snares the legs and trips the rabbit, keeping it from running away so the hunter can catch it.

raid—a sudden attack.

reservation—piece of land set aside by the government for Native Americans to live on.

sacred—spiritual or religious.

sash—a wide piece of cloth used like a belt.

urban—having to do with a city.

ONLINE RESOURCES

Booklinks
NONFICTION NETWORK
FREE! ONLINE NONFICTION RESOURCES

To learn more about the Hopi, please visit **abdobooklinks.com** or scan this QR code. These links are routinely monitored and updated to provide the most current information available.

Index